KING TUT'S

CURSE!

Author:
Jacqueline Morley studied English at Oxford University. She has taught English and History, and now works as a freelance writer. She has written historical fiction and non-fiction for children.

Artist:
David Antram was born in Brighton, England, in 1958. He studied at Eastbourne College of Art and then worked in advertising for fifteen years before becoming a full-time artist. He has illustrated many children's non-fiction books.

Editor:
Karen Smith

Created by:
David Salariya

Published in Great Britain in 2006 by
Book House, an imprint of
The Salariya Book Company Ltd
25 Marlborough Place, Brighton BN1 1UB

S A L A R I Y A

Please visit the Salariya Book Company at:
www.salariya.com
www.book-house.co.uk

ISBN-10: 1-905638-12-4 (HB)   1-905638-13-2 (PB)
ISBN-13: 978-1-905638-12-3 (HB)   978-1-905638-13-0 (PB)

A catalogue record for this book is available from the British Library.

Printed and bound in Belgium.
Printed on paper from sustainable forests.

KING TUT'S CURSE!

WRITTEN BY
JACQUELINE MORLEY

ILLUSTRATED BY
DAVID ANTRAM

CREATED AND DESIGNED BY
DAVID SALARIYA

BOOK HOUSE

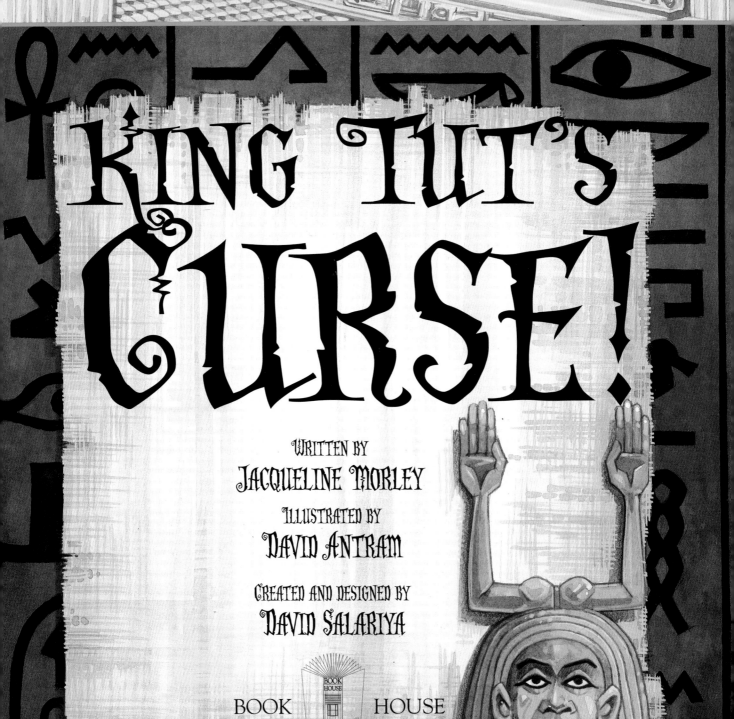

Contents

Introduction

In 1922 two Englishmen uncovered a flight of steps leading to the burial place of an ancient Egyptian king, or pharaoh. They broke through a sealed door and found the body of the king, surrounded by immense treasure, lying in a solid gold coffin. He had been undisturbed for over three thousand years. The men were Lord Carnarvon, a rich aristocrat keen on finding ancient Egyptian remains, and Howard Carter, the archaeologist he hired to help him. Their discovery made newspaper headlines worldwide. Many readers were fascinated by the odd-looking gods and mysterious writing of ancient Egypt. When the people who had been in the tomb died unexpectedly it was claimed they were victims of an ancient curse on anyone who disturbed the pharaoh. Could this be true?

Let's look at the evidence.

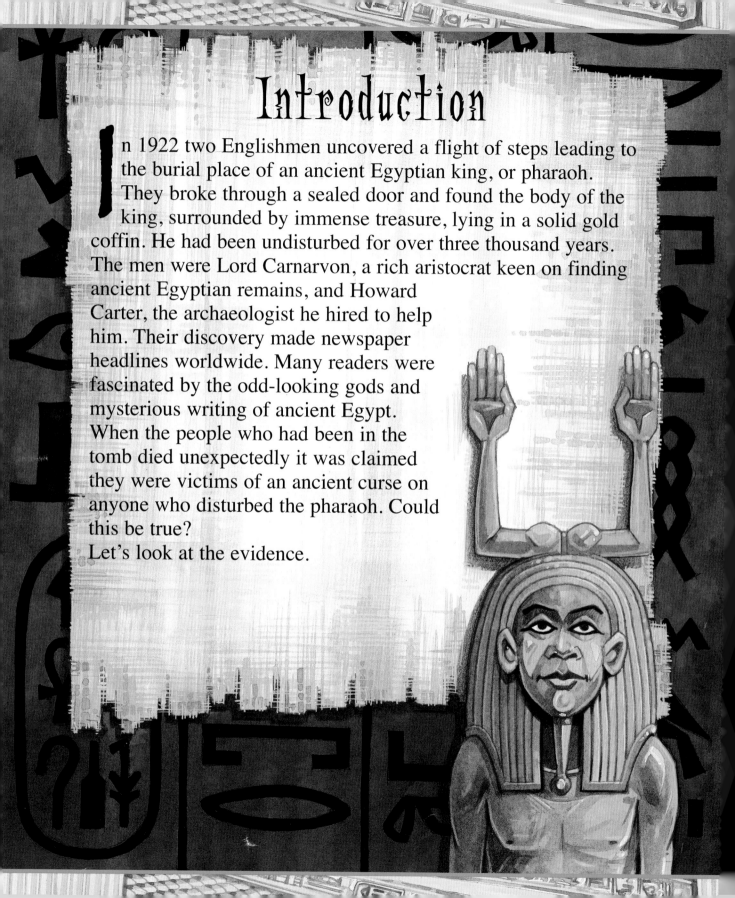

The Boy King

The pharaoh whose tomb was broken into was called Tutankhamun. Very little is known about his reign, which was short and perhaps not very happy. He became king when he was only nine, at a time when things were not going well in Egypt. His father had upset people by forcing them to worship a new god. When he died many officials, especially the priests, saw the chance to undo his work by getting power over the new boy king, who was too young to rule without help. His advisors wanted him to do what suited them. Poor Tutankhamun must have wondered if he could trust anyone.

Hunting (below) in the desert was a royal pastime so the young king may have had some fun like this.

Tutankhamun was married to his half sister. This was quite usual. The pharaohs often married their sisters.

He was only 18 when he died, in 1323 BC – whether through illness, an accident or something sinister, no one knows for sure.

The King Must Live Forever

The boy-king Tutankhamun had not only to rule but to play the part of a god. His people believed that, in some magic way, each of their pharaohs was the son of the sun god, Ra. Through this relationship, Egyptians enjoyed the special favour of the gods. On his death each pharaoh was reunited with the sun god, ensuring that Egypt continued to receive the gods' blessings. This could not happen if the pharaoh's body decayed, for his spirit would perish with it – a dreadful fate which all Egyptians tried to avoid by having their bodies mummified. In the case of a pharaoh this was done with the utmost care, attended by a priest acting the role of the embalmer-god, Anubis.

Stop mumbling! Read the spells out clearly.

Beetle

Amulets

These charms tucked in the linen wrappings, protected the dead pharaoh's spirit. The beetle with open wings, the oval scarab and the eye were all emblems of the sun god.

Scarab

Eye of Ra

8

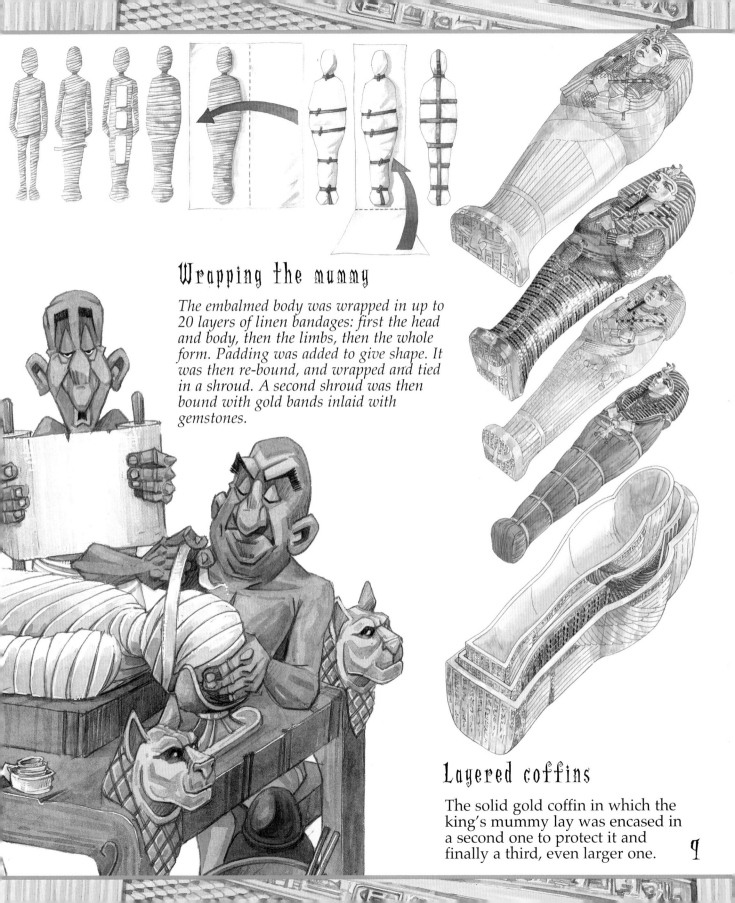

Wrapping the mummy

The embalmed body was wrapped in up to 20 layers of linen bandages: first the head and body, then the limbs, then the whole form. Padding was added to give shape. It was then re-bound, and wrapped and tied in a shroud. A second shroud was then bound with gold bands inlaid with gemstones.

Layered coffins

The solid gold coffin in which the king's mummy lay was encased in a second one to protect it and finally a third, even larger one.

9

Tutankhamun's tomb was in the western hills, for the land of the dead lay in the west. His body went across the Nile from the land of the living on the eastern bank.

The tomb was cut into the slopes of a hidden valley where many pharaohs lay buried. In modern times the area has been named 'The Valley of the Kings'.

To the Land of the Dead

A great procession of priests, courtiers and mourners brought Tutankhamun's coffin to his tomb. Behind came servants bearing goods to be stored in it: food of all types, clothes, furniture, chariots, weapons, model boats, small figures of people – to serve him in the afterlife – and caskets full of fabulous jewellery. These things were for the pharaoh to use in the land of the dead. It seems a magnificent send-off for a pharaoh who hadn't reigned long or done much, but the most famous pharaohs were probably buried with far greater riches. We can't be sure because their tombs were plundered long ago.

Before burial the ceremony of the Opening of the Mouth was held. The new pharaoh, who was also chief priest, touched the mummy with ritual tools and this restored the use of its senses in the aferlife.

Now he's looking a lot more lively!

A Borrowed Tomb?

The Egyptians believed that an undisturbed tomb was a guarantee of immortality. While the body lay there, preserved and protected, its spirit would not perish. Most pharaohs ordered large tombs to be prepared for them well in advance. However, Tutankhamun was buried in one so small that his 'luggage' for the next world would hardly fit in. Perhaps his death was so unexpected that there was no tomb ready and he was placed in someone else's. His mummy, in its three coffins, was set in a magnificent stone sarcophagus covered by four gilded shrines, each encasing the next. Then priests swept away all trace of footprints from the floor and the tomb was sealed, as they thought, forever.

The grave goods were carried down 16 steps, along a sloping passage and into four rooms carved out of the solid rock. After the funeral, all doors except the one to the furthest room, were sealed.

The jackal figure of the god Anubis, preserver of the dead, kept eternal watch over the shrines that held the pharaoh's body.

13

Intruders!

Egyptians knew their pharaohs were buried with lots of treasure and some people were ready to risk the anger of the gods to get it. But there is no record of a thief being struck down by a curse as a result. Many ways of foiling thieves were tried. Some royal tombs had false turns and dangerous pits – but robbers still got in. It may be that the workers who built the tombs were the culprits. Tutankhamun's tomb was broken into and resealed twice, not long after his death. The thieves hurled things about and got away with lots of jewellery. But later, the tomb entrance was accidentally buried by rubble and robberies ceased.

To seal the tomb, the fresh plaster of the blocked-up doorways was stamped with seals like this (above). Its hieroglyphs call for the gods' protection over the tomb.

Officials who cleared up after the robberies only did a quick job. Lots of items were put back in the wrong place.

Robbers may have been caught in the act, for one of them dropped a bundle of rings in his hurry to get out.

Warning!

This hieroglyph shows the fate of tomb robbers. They were killed by being impaled on a stake.

After the first robbery officials blocked the passage with rubble, (above), but the second thieves tunnelled in.

The Valley of the Kings

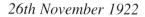

It was not until the 18th century that people realised the Valley of the Kings was the pharaohs' burial place. Then treasure hunters and later, archaeologists, swarmed in. By the 1920s around 60 tombs had been recorded. It seemed there were no more to find, but archaeologist Howard Carter had a hunch that a little-known pharaoh, whose name was on a cup that had been dug up there, must be buried somewhere near. In November 1922 he found some steps and unblocked a passage. Lord Carnarvon, with his daughter and a colleague, Arthur Callender, waited, breathless, as Carter peered through the door at its end.

26th November 1922

In the early 1800s Giovanni Belzoni (above), an adventurer and showman, made many finds in the valley. Careful archaeology developed later.

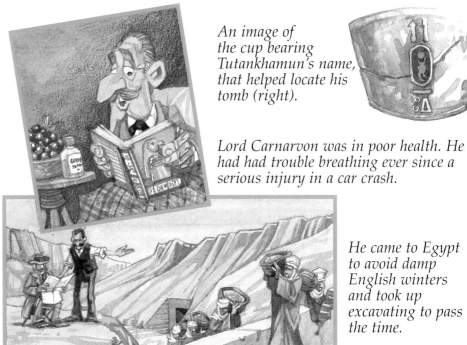

An image of the cup bearing Tutankhamun's name, that helped locate his tomb (right).

Lord Carnarvon was in poor health. He had had trouble breathing ever since a serious injury in a car crash.

He came to Egypt to avoid damp English winters and took up excavating to pass the time.

YES! Wonderful things!

Making Headlines

The discovery was a world sensation. Never before had anyone found a tomb still packed with almost all its contents. It was immediately besieged by reporters, photographers and sightseers hoping to get a glimpse of the incredibly rare objects as they were brought into the daylight. This was a slow process. There were thousands of objects in the tomb and Carter could see that cataloguing and removing each one carefully would take him not just months, but years.

Meanwhile, reporters pestered the archaeologists so much that Carnarvon decided to deal with just one newspaper, *The Times* of London. All news about the finds was given to that newspaper only. But other reporters stayed on in the hot Egyptian sun, displeased at being ignored. Some even tried to 'create' news stories for their newspapers by relying on rumours and guesswork.

It looks divine! But would it be comfortable?

Ignoring the fuss, Carter was busy inside the tomb. Each object was photographed and carefully wrapped before removal to Cairo Museum.

The local telegraph office was overwhelmed by reporters desperate to get their story sent off ahead of their rivals.

Local hotels ran out of rooms and had to accommodate some people in tents in their grounds.

Daily Mail reporter Arthur Weigall had once worked with Carter so he'd expected special treatment and was upset not to get it. He needed news so he encouraged rumours. Weigall claimed later that, seeing Carnarvon going very cheerily into the tomb one day, he'd said to a friend, "If he goes down in that spirit I give him three weeks to live".

Lord Carnarvon Dies

Just over four months later Lord Carnarvon was dead, from an infected mosquito bite (some reports hinted he'd been bittten while in the tomb). By now, the tomb was old news and the unexpected death of Carnarvon was a story readers lapped up. Reports included (untrue) hints about strange omens and a curse. People wrote to newspapers claiming that the priests of ancient Egypt had possessed mystic powers. But in reality there was no mystery about the death.

Did something just bite me?

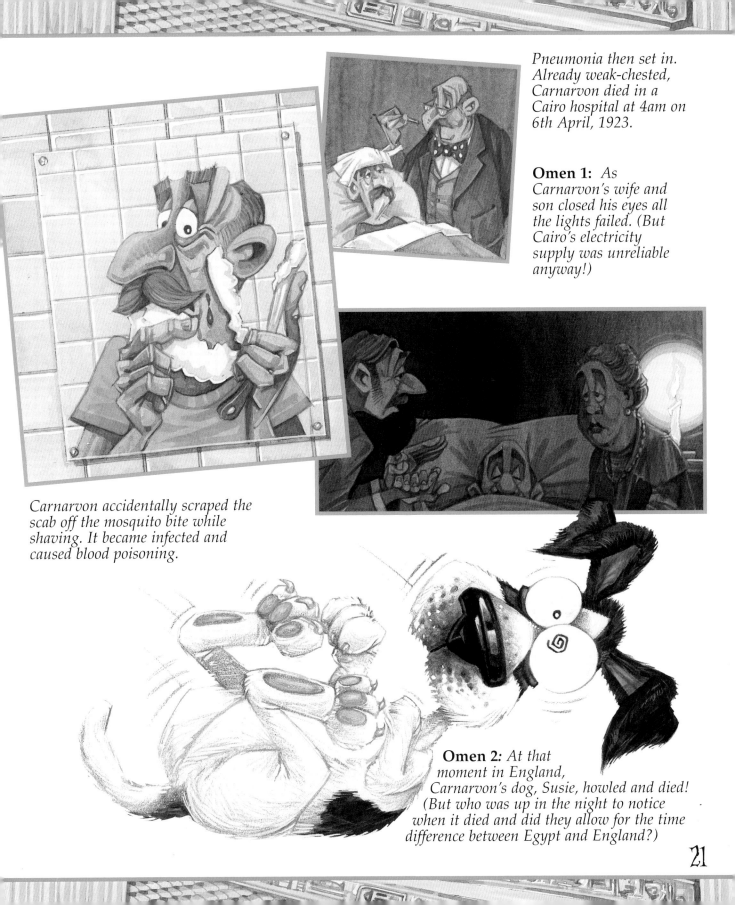

Pneumonia then set in. Already weak-chested, Carnarvon died in a Cairo hospital at 4am on 6th April, 1923.

Omen 1: As Carnarvon's wife and son closed his eyes all the lights failed. (But Cairo's electricity supply was unreliable anyway!)

Carnarvon accidentally scraped the scab off the mosquito bite while shaving. It became infected and caused blood poisoning.

Omen 2: At that moment in England, Carnarvon's dog, Susie, howled and died! (But who was up in the night to notice when it died and did they allow for the time difference between Egypt and England?)

The Fate of a Canary

It's reported that, sometime around the discovery of the steps leading to the tomb, Howard Carter's pet canary was eaten by a cobra. If it was, no one took any notice at the time, but later, when the press started its 'curse of the pharaoh' campaign, the story became big news. According to Arther Weigall, local people hired by Carter to dig at the site were sure this was Tutankhamun's vengeance on the disturber of his tomb. The cobra goddess, Wadjit, appears on Tutankhamun's headdress, rearing herself to spit fire on his enemies.

As soon as the steps were found, Carter rushed to send a telegram to Carnarvon. As Carter entered his tent he saw a cobra eating his canary.

One day an assistant was sent by Carter to get something from his house. He found a coiled cobra in the canary cage!

Could a snake as big as a cobra really squeeze through the bars of a canary cage? Yes! In the 1990s, a TV team making a programme about the tomb did an experiment with a cobra and a canary, to find out. They barely had time to save the canary!

A year later Carter asked a friend to look after his canary. Could it have been the same canary supposedly eaten by the snake, or did he buy another?

22

The Rumours Grow

Newspapers loved the curse story and the story grew. People started remembering, or thought they were remembering, signs that had foretold Carnarvon's doom. One of the most popular stories was about the curse said to have been found in the tomb. Some said it was written on a wall, others on an object of some type. In fact, no curse was found on anything, but even sensible people really believed they had seen it. A young anthropologist and his university tutor, shown around by Carter, recollected being struck by an inscription over the door: 'Death to those who enter'.

Marie Corelli, a romantic novelist blamed ancient poisons in the tomb for Carnarvon's death.

THE CURSE OF OSIRIS

Superstition Surrounds Carnarvon's Death

MARIE CORELLI'S POISON THEORY

Fortune teller 'Velma' said he'd warned of deadly peril awaiting Carnarvon, after reading his palm. Velma sketched the lines of Carnarvon's hand (left).

The British Museum received a flurry of parcels containing statuettes and bits of mummy, sent by panicked collectors anxious to avoid a curse.

The 'mummy's curse' featured in books and films long before the Tutankhamun craze, but the rumours about his tomb gave it a big boost.

25

The Death Toll Rises

The curse of Tutankhamun was such a good story that newspapers were keen to keep it going. The death of anyone remotely connected with the tomb was reported in spooky terms suggesting the curse was still at work. Yet the 'curse' missed obvious targets. The 12 experts most closely involved with the tomb (including Lord Carnarvon) survived for an average of 23 years.

Carnarvon's daughter, one of the first to enter the tomb, lived until 1980.

Carter should have been the prime candidate for the curse, as he spent long hours working on Tutankhamun's coffins. The coffins were stuck together by hardened resin and he painstakingly chipped it off. Yet Carter lived until 1939.

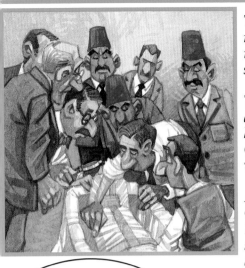

The ten people present as the mummy was actually unwrapped (left) were all still alive nine years later.

The Director of Antiquities at the Louvre collapsed of heat stroke at the tomb (right) and died. BUT he was 69.

Arthur Mace (right), one of Carter's assistant died in 1928. BUT he had been suffering from heart, chest and lung problems.

An Egyptian prince, Ali Fahmy Bey (right), was shot by his wife in a London hotel, after visiting the tomb. Whatever her reasons were, the curse was blamed.

I wonder if the pharaoh minds us doing this?

In 1929 a very unlucky chain of events made 'curse' headlines. Carter's secretary died (in London, of heart failure). His elderly father, overcome by the news, fell from a 7th floor window. Later, his funeral hearse ran over a small boy on the way to the cemetery. If that was Tutankhamun's vengeance, it seems very unreasonable of him!

27

The Real Victim

If opening the pharaoh's tomb has harmed anyone, it is Tutankhamun himself. Carter unwrapped the mummy to examine the body. A photograph was taken and Tutankhamun was returned to his coffin. But the photo hid the fact that the body was by then in several pieces.

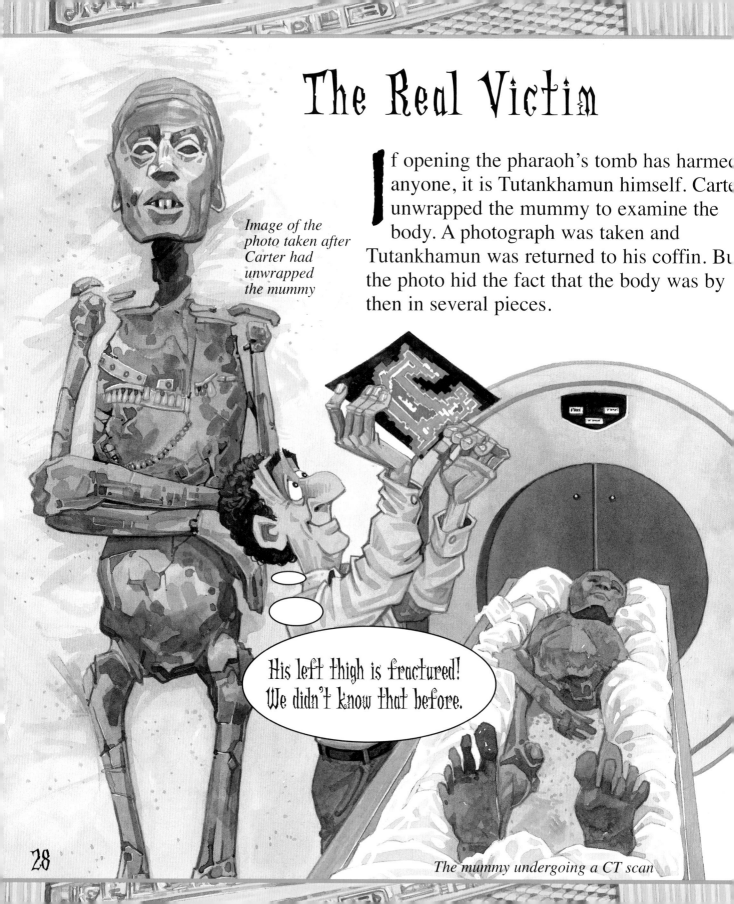

Image of the photo taken after Carter had unwrapped the mummy

His left thigh is fractured! We didn't know that before.

The mummy undergoing a CT scan

The true damage to the body was revealed in 1968 when it was taken out for X-ray. Carter had not been able to get the body out of the coffin whole because of hardened resin around it, so he had taken it to pieces. Tutankhamun was disturbed again for X-ray in 1978 and for a CT scan in 2005 and more bits of him have broken off. What a fate for an ancient Egyptian, who believed that without a complete body his spirit would die.

X-raying Tutankhamun, 1968 (below). It was found that his breastbone and part of his ribcage were missing.

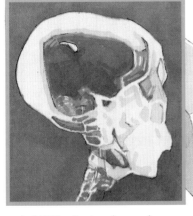

The 1968 x-ray showed a chip of bone inside the king's skull. This suggested he'd had a head injury, but now it is thought Howard Carter himself may have done the damage.

A 1978 photo showed more damage. The eye sockets have sunk, the eyelids are gone and the right ear is missing (left).

There may be real hazards in tombs rather than curses. Archaeologists now wear masks to protect against micro-organisms.

Glossary

Anthropologist A person who studies the science of the development of mankind.

Belzoni, Giovanni (1778-1823) An Italian man hired by an English collector to hunt for Egyptian antiquities. He had an amazing knack for finding tombs. Although basically a treasure hunter, he laid the foundation for the science of Egyptology.

Blood poisoning A condition in which harmful bacteria from an infection invade the blood stream, causing very high fever.

Carnarvon, George Herbert, 5th Earl of (1866-1923) A wealthy Englishman who began excavating to pass the time. He became hooked, even though in his first year all he found was a mummified cat. Realising he didn't really know where to dig, he hired a specialist: Howard Carter

Carter, Howard (1874-1939) An archaeologist who had no university training. He came to Egypt at the age of 17 as a draughtsman and learnt on the job. He was a careful and conscientious worker, giving the rest of his life to studying the tomb and its contents.

CT scan A type of X-ray that produces a three-dimensional image.

Embalmer A person whose trade is the preservation of bodies.

Hieroglyphs Signs representing words, syllables or sounds, that formed the Egyptian alphabet.

Immortality The ability to live forever.

Jackal African and Asian animal of the dog family.

Micro-organisms Living things invisible to the naked eye, such as bacteria and mould spores.

Nile The very long river that flows northwards through Egypt.

Omen Something regarded as a sign of future disaster.

Resin A sticky substance obtained from trees.

Ritual tools Tools used in a religious ceremony.

Sarcophagus An outer coffin made of stone.

Scarab A dung beetle.

Seal An engraved object used to stamp an official mark into soft wax or plaster on a door, letter or container. It then cannot be opened without the seal being broken.

Shrine A construction enclosing a sacred object.

Shroud A wrapping for a corpse.

Telegraph office Place for sending messages long-distance, instantly, from an electric transmitter to a receiver which printed them out.

Telegram Message sent by telegraph.

Tutankhamun Pharaoh of the 18th dynasty (family of rulers) who ruled Egypt from 1333 to 1323 BC.

Note: The 12 experts most closely involved with the tomb of Tutankhamun (see page 26) were: Howard Carter, Lord Carnarvon, Arthur Callender, Arthur Mace, Arthur Lucas, Henry Burton, Percy Newberry, James Breasted, Alan Gardner, Douglas Derry, Lindsley Foote Hall and Walter Hauser.

Index

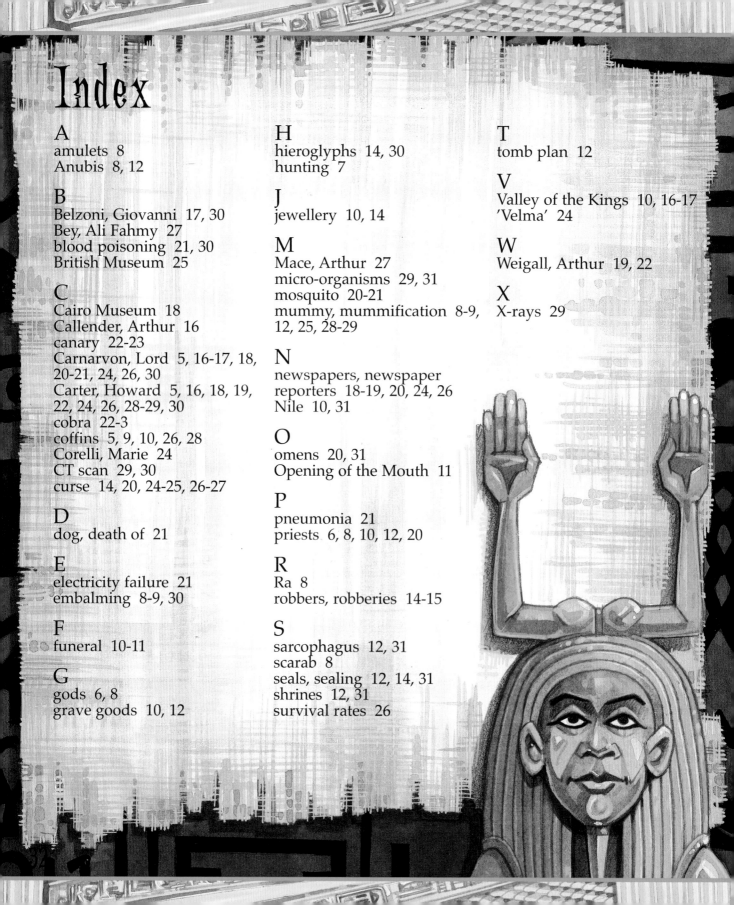